A WILD REGION

A WILD REGION

poems & paintings KATE BUCKLEY

foreword by CECILIA WOLOCH

April 2008

A Wild Region
Copyright 2008 by Kate Buckley

Graphic design
Michael Wada

Editors
Ricki Mandeville
Michael Miller

Moon Tide logo design
Ricki Mandeville

A Wild Region
is published by
Moon Tide Press
Anaheim, CA
www.moontidepress.com

FIRST EDITION

Printed in the United States of America

ISBN 1-60585-233-1

for Gran –
for your wit, wisdom, warmth,
and above all, love.

In Memoriam

Christine Shouse Dummit, 1905 – 2007

Contents

Foreword

The wild region of Kate Buckley's poems is a region my own heart knows well. I also have roots in rural Kentucky, and complicated ties to that landscape, lush and haunted as it is. So it's little wonder these poems break my heart, though I think they would break anyone's. Written with both tenderness and precision, they pay homage to that wild region in each of us — lost and unreachable, ruined and beautiful — and to the home that is always present in the exile's heart, as the past is always present in us, as are our dead beloveds, who still call us back to that home, that ground.

Kate Buckley's poems are dark prayers and lyrical ballads, infused with mystery and awe, respectful of the hard lives lived in the wild region the poet has left behind but still carries within her. She lifts them up, those lost beloveds, so that the dead may speak in her poems, and the hills and valleys and slow running streams. This is how suffering is made to mean, how human lives are woven into the landscape in which they're lived, how the voiceless are given voice — "songs for the mountains/ hummed for the lost." And the stories these poems tell — finely crafted as the poems are — are stories that speak to all of us, accessible and clear for all their complicated depth, "universal" precisely because they're so deeply personal, and so deeply felt.

And yet Buckley never strays into sentimentality, and never ties anything up too neatly. She renders this world in clear, vivid detail, and in language that's starkly lyrical:

> the coughs that stained your linens black
> no matter how many times you bleached them back
> by the creek where you caught crawdads for supper.

and she allows the beauty and terror of this world to shine through the pictures she paints with words:

> You made a kite for me once, weaving far into the night
> a red tailed hawk with scarlet ribbons streaming like entrails
> against the gray Kentucky sky.
> ("Laurel County")

Almost every poem ends in an even deeper sense of mystery than it began, often with a quiet awe at what has happened, what keeps happening; an ever-deepening hush. In "When We Were Young," the speaker re-imagines her parents, dancing to jazz late at night:

> I saw them once
> moving slowly into each other
> against the pale August night,
> his dark hand on her shoulder,
> her laughter, the brightest sound
> I have ever known,
> sailing up and over
> lighting every candle in the room.

There is so much stunning language in this collection, so much accuracy and grace, and there are so many images that take my breath away, that I'm tempted to quote from the poems at length, but I'm also hesitant to take anything out of its context. So inextricably interwoven are the lives Buckley illuminates here with the landscape she paints, so deftly does she move us through time, that I would urge the reader to begin at the beginning and read straight through, following the trajectory the poems make deeper and deeper into the heart of things.

In an age when so much poetry is self-referential to the point of excluding the reader, this is poetry that includes, that matters, and that, in breaking the heart, opens it. In "A Poem of Strong Wishes," the poet describes a last visit with a dying grandmother:

> over and over she wonders
>
> why I left Kentucky;
> another time she says
> *this place is such a mess*
>
> over and over,
> until I lay hands on her bird bones

and whisper

sshh
the way you do to the wind
or a very small child,

and then I say *Gran, it's beautiful,*
everything is beautiful.
...
You can go now
if you want.

Kate Buckley shows us how the beautiful and the brutal can not only coexist alongside one another, but exist within one another. Hers is a necessary and welcome new voice.

— Cecilia Woloch

The people of the wild regions of Kentucky may have learned some of the arts of peace, and get their livings by more or less regular industry in simple forms, such as tilling the soil and distilling moonshine whisky. But they are none the less unreclaimed savages, and the work of civilizing and Christianizing them must begin from the beginning if it is ever to be accomplished at all.

The New York Times, July 9, 1885

As the machines come and the people go
the old names rise, chattering, and depart.

Wendell Berry, "The Record"

The Road Home

Times I wake from dreams,
transported from fields and winding roads,
seasons so bright you'd bite
the insides of your cheeks
until they bled – a swift, sharp slice,
clean and simple.

Easy to forget in this age of constant apocalypse,
this place of buildings breeding faster than rabbits,
where I do not grow my food
or know my neighbor.

I have ridden on horseback
under the harvest moon, gold and heavy –
a buck's moon, another world.

I have tramped bramble and goldenrod,
through stalactites of birch,
icy creeks and rocky passes,
dog at my heel, sky spreading for miles.

I carry within me hymns of my mothers,
stories of my fathers, encoded in blood,
woven in hair, etched in bend of bone,
in this place of memory and metaphor,
of hills and valleys,
of slow running streams.

Black Mountain Pantoum

We climbed Black Mountain in the rain,
the coal-dark rain of diamonds
long since dissipated,
staining our skin a slow black.

The coal-dark rain of diamonds,
feet seeking purchase up thin side of hill,
staining our skin a slow black,
dusky trickles, small rivers of the body.

Feet seeking purchase up thin side of hill,
trees' roots cracking like bird bones,
dusky trickles, small rivers of the body
beneath sagging soot of foothill.

Trees' roots cracking like bird bones,
mountain cleaved of stomach
beneath sagging soot of foothill,
stripped clean of veins.

Mountain cleaved of stomach,
long since dissipated,
stripped clean of veins,
we climbed Black Mountain in the rain.

Looking Glass

Laurel County

There must have been times
Kentucky seemed a life sentence,
a dark-veined monster burning coal in her belly,

the coughs that stained your linens black
no matter how many times you bleached them back
by the creek where you caught crawdads for supper.

You tell me of life but do not mention hunger,
you speak instead of land: tramping the fields in the wake of your father,
finding a fishing hole or story, and the last time you saw him,

Pappaw told you how Granddaddy got killed by a train,
cut in two on his way to the Hensley place –
this, during Prohibition, and a man did what he could.

Your mother canned beans and berries
from the share-cropped fields behind the house.
I remember the jam, thick and expensive on Wonder Bread.

I never understood why you'd fix me with thundercloud eyes
if I did not finish my piece,
your Cherokee granny's picture glaring from the other room.

You made a kite for me once, weaving far into the night
a red tailed hawk with scarlet ribbons streaming like entrails
against the gray Kentucky sky.

I ran and ran,
legs fighting my lungs –
could not let it fall.

You were on the hilltop – skirt taut,
caught between your legs, signaling something,
I could not make out what,

the kite obscuring my vision –
the wind would catch it, then let it fall.

After the Famine
– Maysville, 1865

There were shadows in the woods,
creatures who watched him on his long walk
home from the mill

he worked every day save Sunday,
grinding the grain against giant rocks, smooth,
as finely gauged as the inner workings of a woman.

He walked most nights alone,
stark figure stalking through bluegrass and birch trees,
lone stands of white warriors dotting the savannah.

He once heard footsteps though he never saw a figure,
his setter growling, harsh brush of hair rising on his back;
the dog slept inside after that.

Elizabeth waiting for him with floured hands, soft aching flesh;
their third child asleep in the hewn cradle at their feet,
they made their fourth.

They built a life by the river,
growing what they could
in this rock-ribbed place of lakes and streams,

a long way from the loughs and cottages,
raw turnips, men sucking blood from cattle,
Irish skeletons carried over on coffin ships,

corpses piled like cords of wood,
spilling into the harbor,
shadows of the sea.

After the Fall

Winter now, crops put away,
fields heavy with snow,
jagged limestone jutting out of the ice
like so many stars on their way to heaven.

She stands at the door to the cabin,
hand to her belly, her best muslin straining
over her seventh, and last.

She follows him down the path,
touching each stone as they pass,
willing the rocks to bless them,
to keep them safe from harm.

She watches him as they stand
side-by-side in the small, still room
between the mud-chinked walls.

His overalls still dark
despite their many washings, his eyes spark
though he has not slept in many nights –
she wonders if he will see their child.

Their voices lift over the back of a song,
slide along its keening spine

like the wind in autumn through bare-boned trees,
like the last few days before the snows.

Stars on Their Way

Mt. Eden
– Shelby County, 1912

Her name was Matt and she was dear and good,
loved me as I loved her.

Dark as a night with no moon and no stars,
and slow sometimes. Languid,

the way she moved, the way she spoke,
like water when it has no wind

and no reason to move,
and so stays where it falls.

Always she'd eat in the kitchen after we'd finished
and I'd slip in to sit beside her;

she'd make us cambric tea:
hot water, sugar, lots of cream.

I'd go with her to clean the colored church
most Sundays, and she'd push my carriage

with the red-fringed parasol
up the bumpy country road to Mt. Eden.

I sat in the shadows of the little church
while her voice played among the rafters

and her hands, swift as angels' wings,
flew among the pews.

One day she was not there at breakfast
and my mother said she'd married the Baptist minister and left us.

I waited for her for days,
waited for her soft, slow step,

the deep, clear pond of her voice,
her good, calm hands, but she never came.

When I was older, my mother said the man Matt married
got tired of her, got rid of her, poisoned her tea,

wrapped her up like a sack of kittens,
weighted her swollen body with a stone,

pushed her over the bank in the cool, dark night,
then a long, slow journey to the bottom of the pond.

Appalachia

(for R.M., 1893 – 1947)

Turkey-red patchwork covers my bed,
muslin nightshirt, yellow with age,

deeds of trust, death and marriage
rusted in an old lock box.

Deep in the hollows, far in the shadows,
under the thickets, beyond train tracks,

past corn fields, through cotton,
down through the caves —

mechanics and coalminers,
dusky farmers of the underbelly of my birth,

girl of trickle-down stories, hand-me-down shoes,
coal dust, the curse of black lung,

racing the sun down the long corridor
of the last train out.

Dulcimers, button boxes,
quilts from aprons and rags,

song for the day,
dirge for the night,

crooning soft and low
over dime store light,

songs for the mountains
hummed for the lost,

words that beat behind my eyes,
melodies that haunt my sleep –

the rumbling long before midnight
and the woman who found you

broken
beneath the last train out.

Pink Moon

Coming Down Fall

She lives near where she was born,
long valley in the eastern hills,

dusty-patched town snaking through rills
and streams, dribbling down rocks,

falling into leaves where they stay
burrowing back to ground, waiting winter.

She clerks at the auto parts store
where her husband was mechanic,

'til the day the Buick fell,
crushing him against cement,

his spine crumbling like scree,
his screams sending even the rats from their holes.

She lies each night in the bed where she was born,
covered with her grandmother's quilts,

patchworked with the fabrics of firsts and lasts:
christening, communion, wedding gown –

from birth to burial, they snug around her sleeping form,
waiting, waiting, pulling at her bones;

the stitches of her eyes, yarn of her mouth,
worn fabric of the body,

winter waiting at the walls.

Harlan County

Stepping over the stones of my mother,
chicken bones, straw,

the cellar in which the man was found,
that man my grandfather

the day the sharecroppers left town,
their son shot dead –

the things whiskey'll do to a man.

The woman who waited under the house at night,
counting ghosts and bobcats through lattice of leaves,

walking bare-boned lanes,
toes buried beneath blackened leaves –

no cause for worry
if you've walked every acre, planted every row.

Nothing can get you if you pay it no mind.

I tell you these things
so you'll not mistake my actions for fear,

not think I do not know what makes a life,
what makes people do the things they do.

I know my fears – I've named them,
counted them out one by one

like tarot cards, voodoo dolls:

birth,
death,
poverty,
obscurity,
that you will leave me,
or I will leave you.

Blood on the Moon

Ballad of Walking Alone

She never meant to do it,
but there are seeds sown deep that green and bud
and one day flower. As day follows night
these things come to pass.

She never thought herself capable of such an act,
despite her genealogy of horse-thieves and train-tracks.
She was well acquainted with sackcloth and ashes,
said scripture backward on third full moons,
knew what to do when a spider bit you
or a man you didn't want
had his way with you.

She knew rue and comfort, rosemary,
and the small spindly insects
that cooked in oil,
produce a satisfying crunch.

She walked for miles to set a leg,
stayed up half the night
when the mad woman cut herself,
had to be sewn back together –
skin bunching at the seams,
needle darting through thin, frayed flesh.

It was black the night it happened,
barely a sliver hold of moon,
pennyworth of stars, slick chill wind
driving the hairs on her neck,
setting her feet to home.

There was a man,
hands hanging like hands,
waist like the trunk of a tree,
eyes glinting flint-cold, steel-hard
like the eyes of an animal when it is cornered,
has no option but to attack.

As he saw it, she'd killed him already –
turned his woman against him,
cut his child from her fading womb,
hidden them both away,
then one tiny grave, one rail ticket to somewhere
he'd never heard of, wouldn't go to even if he had.

He believed in vengeance – washed his face with it,
drank it down, sharpened his claws on the shards
of the small, brown bottles.

He would have killed her too
only she saw him first –
read his mind the way she would the tracks of an animal,
raised her gun and fired.

They drowned her next morning,
even after his pockets spilled out
her letters to his wife,
a ticket stub, and a knife.

She gave no argument —
she'd known death for quite a while.
She'd known her life's end
lay at the bottom of a well,

the moon caught hanging in the shadows,
a silver cobwebbed veil.

Rue

Sun filters through skeleton palms,
dank water licks lazily at shoreline,
tortoises sleep their green hill dreams.

Swampland sings its stuck-mud staccato,
shaded path winds around the lake
over and over to its starting place,

the way a road takes us
where we no longer want to go.

Repentance does not undo what has been done,
and grass tramped by heavy boots
soon springs back.

There is truth in vengeance,
in the flowering over and over
of evil deeds

until they have gone to seed,
withered in hoarfrost ground.

American Bethlehem

I tore her out of my body,
gave her milk-blood from my flesh,
wove rivulets through floorboards with pacing,
quieted her demons, quelled the shadows –
her angry face to mine
and I did not know her.

She came to me strangely –
the last person I expected to see.

That afternoon behind the barn,
his red hands and knotted sex –
I know with certainty, this is
my punishment.

I sit behind closed doors,
back to the wall, knees drawn to my chin,
eyes closed, and I pray,
though I've forgotten how to ask for things.

I watch her sleeping, lashes blue against rounded cheeks
and I can't breathe for wishing.

I will give her more than was given me,
I want her to know what I could not:
a life without reprisal,
a world without consequence.

Supplication

Spring

Three babies play at her feet,
dark heads burnished in the mid-March sun.

They are laid out before her,
a small army.

One clings to her skirts, chubby hand clenched in a fist,
beats a tiny tattoo against her plump-veined thigh.

She thinks of life before them,
remembers coffee and quiet,

the dry hills stretched before her,
brown with winter,

seeds buried deep,
waiting for the rains,

for the thick viscous mud,
for the translucence of first small shoots,

for the vines that finally curl and stretch
small fingers to the sun.

American Queen
— *Owensboro*

Two hours leave
off the boat that watches me everywhere,
even on this riverbank where I sit

legs crossed, feet crammed into the only
other pair of shoes I got
and this old man's watching me

like he wants something
only I got nothing.

Two hours leave
and I'm not going to waste it
on an old man with no teeth.

I stare over the graying skyline,
rocked by the shadows of the boat,
sprawling, immense, eclipsing

even the yawning bridges
with graffiti in their teeth.

"A tarted-up cake," my momma said.
"New Orleans on a bad day," laughed my sister.
"But it *moves*," I said.

And in two hours will carry me
farther away
from this still, silent backwater

that goes nowhere
and smells of it too.

Solitude

A Sunday Night in Kentucky

One of my legs was longer than the other when I was a child.
Then a man came to our tin-roofed church,
a tall man with open face, kind eyes.

My mother said he'd sandy hair
and I searched for gritty particles
where his hair parted like the red sea,

below that, his eyes: green with specks like seaweed;
an iridologist told me those meant the body was impure –
no small irony as this man was a healer.

He sat me down, back to the pock-marked wall,
brown legs, knotted knees stiff out in front,
a jack-knifed doll, an experiment.

His hands were warm as he held my face,
breathed into my mouth, filling the air with strange sounds,
a kind of incantation, incarnation:

Jesus we praise you, you are here in this place,
you are here with this child, and we thank you Jesus,

Jesus we ask you to heal her leg – cause her right leg, Jesus,
to meet her left; Jesus you promise these things if we believe,

if we hear your voice, and Father, hallelujah,
we believe and she believes;

Father send your Holy Spirit into this place,
let us see your power and grace,

let us see this leg grow, Father,
grow, Father, thank you, Lord Jesus.

I arose at his invitation and walked the room,
sat back down and someone got a ruler.
The yellow tape spilled down my thigh, curled around my toes.
I stretched my legs in front of me. Women were crying;
the man thanked Jesus for a miracle.
A hot tear fell on my tangled hands and I realized it was mine.

As I grew, my legs resumed their own peculiar rhythm,
forgot Jesus, moved away,
walked beaches instead of country roads.

Still, there are times when the moon is full,
the house empty and shuttered with regret,
that I think of the night

when I stood straight as an arrow
pointing to heaven.

By the Lake

By the lake, after supper,
ashes raked smooth, voices roiling in the distance,
I move silently, swiftly,
weaving through pines on small unsteady legs,
following the pale stream of light,
racing the shadows.

I am a collector of secrets and cobwebs,
dreams jumbled with half-remembered images,
staccato words thrumming at my temples,
small points of thunder.

His ruddy hand, her waist a small whiteness,
forming continents – a geography for which I had no name,
my tongue too big for my mouth,
sounds spilling to my throat.

Running out from dark pines, bursting to the light,
ascending the hill at the last lick of day,
green flash on the horizon,
pale hillocks breaking at my feet –
the white grass of summer
shelter for lacebugs and crickets,

the smell of night opening around me
like my mother's evening bag spilling out
its secret perfume – an aura of forbidden places,
an awakening.

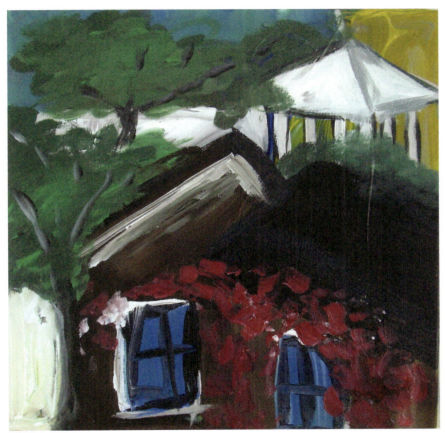

The Lake House

My Mother's Closet

I had a fascination with your dresses – the greens, brocades,
the belted shapes which spoke of you more poignantly
than the photos in their careful frames.

Your shoes were their own country, the heels, satins,
the inexplicable mud – I scraped them with small fingernails,
marveling at the gorgeous debris, wishing I had a microscope.

I searched your handbags, examined them for signs,
evidence – where you were going, where you had been:
tickets, lipstick, inked hieroglyphics, a broken comb.

I even smelled your stockings, sniffing at the crotches
like a dog, frantic for any trace of you, my eyes raking
their length, wondering at ladders, searching for clues.

My father came upon me once, cross-legged on the floor,
his sad smile telling me more than any detection –
he took my hand, and closed the door.

When We Were Young

I was always the darker one,
dusky as a gypsy my Granny said,
with cat-colored eyes,
legs longer than was good for me,
always bruised from climbing trees,

my sister, china eyed,
skin paler than any moon –
smooth as the jazz
our parents played late at night
after we'd gone to bed.

I saw them once
moving slowly into each other
against the pale August night,
his dark hand on her shoulder,
her laughter, the brightest sound
I have ever known,
sailing up and over
lighting every candle in the room.

A Letter on the Counter

There were no men in the trees today,
no moths by the pale moon of the kitchen light,
phosphorescent in the morning mist of frozen ground, yawning valley,
no sign that life was still the life we knew —

the weeping of cicadas, the muted thud of horses' hooves,
the clatter of men in the orchards
filling their arms with golden fruit,
burlap sacks yawning on the earth beneath;

no noises in the kitchen,
no hiss of bacon, hum of teapot,
not even the dog makes a sound as he looks up from his bed,
thumps his stubby tail, closes his eyes.

This is the sound of absence,
the secret of betrayal simply this:
she was there one day,
and then she was not.

After Eden

The Politics of Wanting

The government of lost souls,
the language of loneliness;
there is never enough.
She knows that now.

The man she married
leaves his keys in the door
as if planning an escape route
should he wake in the middle of the night,
look over at her sleeping form,
decide his heart cannot last another day.

In the mornings he makes her coffee,
a small offering of peace.

Weeks go by without their touching;
moving past one another in hallways
they apologize for a brushed arm, elbow,
the hanging sorrow of a love grown cold.

She watches him with the horses,
how he grips their manes, racing the long broad sky.
He looks at her strangely;
she wonders if he can read her mind.

The vicious pruning of time,
the inept metaphor of sleep,
the grass-green beauty
of the way she moves beneath him
as he wills himself to other lands.

On Hearing Your News

My eyes lie flat in my skull,
darkened, bruised

lashes whip-stitched to swollen lids –
sleep has once again been elusive.

My organs weigh more
than they did the day before,

swollen with unhappiness,
gorged on regret:

tiny fists in my stomach pummeling
the hanging ball of my heart.

Miner's Pond

At Miner's Pond we use the past
to pull ourselves forward; rowing.
        – Anne Michaels

I sit on the bank, hand on dog's domed head,
finger the copper curls blazing in the last hour of daylight.
We are waiting for release.

There are faded vines still clinging to the hillside,
breathless sun choking dust-strewn air,
motes swimming in August sky.

We are waiting for the haunting that fades
come September, chill chasing away fetid mist,
whorls like damp ghosts in flattened grasses,

leaving behind nothing so much as sap singing,
scarlet creeping through every vein,
until at last we crawl to the shore and sleep.

Christine

A Poem of Strong Wishes

I live at the end of the world
free to come and go at will,
the shore the only thing binding me

and the last time I saw Grandmother
she said such funny things –
over and over she wonders

why I left Kentucky;
another time she says
this place is such a mess

over and over,
until I lay hands on her bird bones
and whisper

sshh
the way you do to the wind
or a very small child,

and then I say *Gran, it's beautiful,*
everything is beautiful.
I wish and whisper in her spun-floss hair

as fine as any dandelion
You can go now
if you want.

Flying back to the shore
I think that none of us are free
bound as we are

by promises outliving us all,
the grasping at things
pulling us in and out of worlds.

Last Visit

I cradle her, cradle her in my arms
such a frail thing, muscles shrunk to tendrils
barely covering bones,
I sing her songs she sang to me.

Such a frail thing, muscles shrunk to tendrils
heart still remembering to beat,
I sing her songs she sang to me,
smooth her wispy hair, fine as floss,

heart still remembering to beat.
I kiss the space between her eyes,
smooth her wispy hair, fine as floss
cotton against the pale earth of her skull.

I kiss the space between her eyes,
the membranes pale and shrunken,
cotton against the pale earth of her skull.
I pray to every god I've ever known.

The membranes pale and shrunken
barely covering bones,
I pray to every god I've ever known,
I cradle her, cradle her, and rock her home.

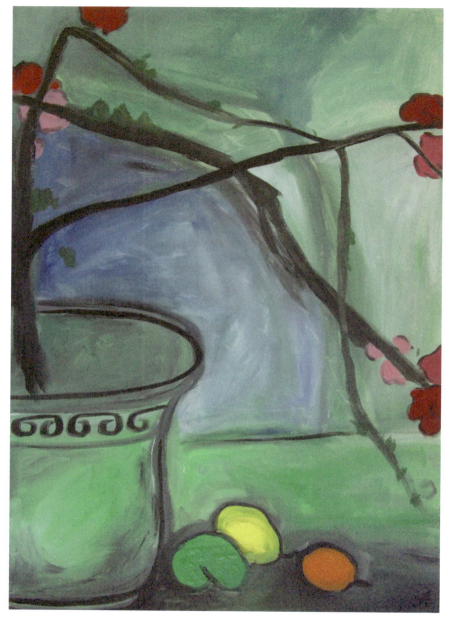

The Veranda

Last Supper

My father's mother's mother saw 102 winters,
missing only her last spring.

I do not think she'd mind,
trapped as she's been these many years,

hanging in the balance of day and night,
dependent upon every spoonful, every drop.

She was buried today in a garden in Kentucky,
celebrated cemetery amidst the frozen fields,

laid to her husband's right, the waiting stone fed,
the yawning dash closed like a bookend.

Tonight I feel the mourning set in,
feel it draw its lines and dig in deep;

in protest, I prepare her favorite repast:
cold chicken, cheddar cheese, crackers, a glass of wine.

I make her a cracker the way she likes it,
offer her a sip of my *fancy-schmancy* wine.

No one is here to see this,
and the dogs do not mind.

I unearth letters, photos, tell her how wonderful she is –
a grand lady, everyone says, *the end of an era,* my ex-husband says.

She is, but she is more.
She is the reason I know how kindness sounds: rich, throaty, warm.

She is the reason I talk to myself,
why I do not fear winter,

why things take root in me
and sometimes bloom.

Acknowledgements

Grateful acknowledgement is made to the editors of the following publications in which versions of these poems first appeared:

The Heartland Review: "When We Were Young"

New Southerner: "Harlan County," "Laurel County"

Slipstream: "The Politics of Wanting"

Spillway: "On Hearing Your News"

Tide Pools: An Anthology of Orange County Poetry: "My Mother's Closet"

My gratitude as well to members of the Laguna Poets Workshop for their support, guidance and encouragement. Many thanks also to Michael Miller and Moon Tide Press for their unflagging belief in me, and tremendous thanks to Ricki Mandeville for her generous editorial support, feedback and friendship. Appreciation and love to my family…in all its incarnations. And to Charles Carstensen, more love than I can say.

About the Author

Kate Buckley's poems have been published in *The Heartland Review, New Southerner, Slipstream* and *Spillway*, among other journals, and in the book *Tide Pools: An Anthology of Orange County Poetry*. She was a 2007 finalist for the Joy Bale Boone Poetry Prize, the 2007 winner of the Gabehart Prize for Imaginative Writing for poetry, and the 2008 winner of the *North American Review's* James Hearst Poetry Prize. Buckley is also a classically trained painter; her work has been privately collected and published in journals such as *The Adirondack Review* and purchased by such entities as the American Institute of Certified Public Accountants. A ninth-generation Kentuckian, educated at Transylvania University and the University of Kentucky, Buckley now lives with her husband in Laguna Beach. *A Wild Region* is her first book.

Index of Images

Printed in the United States
107867LV00002B